DISCUSSION PAPER 68

RECONCEPTUALISING DEMOCRATIC LOCAL GOVERNANCE IN THE NIGER DELTA

SOLOMON T. EBOBRAH

NORDISKA AFRIKAINSTITUTET, UPPSALA 2011

Indexing terms:
Nigeria, Niger Delta
Federalism
Public administration
Decentralization
Local government
Governance
Democratization
Social participation
Petroleum resources
Resource allocation
Community development

*The opinions expressed in this volume are those of the author
and do not necessarily reflect the views of Nordiska Afrikainstitutet.*

Language checking: Peter Colenbrander

ISSN 1104-8417

ISBN 978-91-7106-709-8

Production: Byrå4

Print on demand, Lightning Source UK Ltd.

Contents

Foreword

This Discussion Paper examines the crisis in Nigeria's ethnic-minority oil-producing Niger Delta region from the perspective of the shortcomings of the local government administration system. It provides a broad description of local governance in Nigeria and the Niger Delta, focusing on the conceptual and political basis of local government administration as the third tier of federal administration. This forms the foundation for the critique of the practice of federalism in Nigeria, and underscores the position that the situation in the Niger Delta cannot be understood outside the contradictions of a highly centralised federal system. The Niger Delta is presented as a case where the contradictions of Nigerian federalism are writ large at the local level. This approach yields deep insights into how these shortcomings are manifest in the Niger Delta, and how they impact negatively on governance in the region. The major criticism levelled at local governance in the Niger Delta relates to the lack of democracy in the local administration, a shortcoming further compounded by inadequate funding, poor leadership, the inequitable distribution of the benefits of the oil industry, and the lack of accountability, representation and capacity, all of which deepen the crisis of development in the oil-rich region. Given a local government administration structure that alienates rather than responds to the demands and needs of the people at the grassroots in the Niger Delta, the author makes a case for the genuine democratisation of local governance based on participation of the people of the region. What is clearly demonstrated is that existing local governments in the region cannot be agents of democratic transformation and that transformation cannot take place outside a national process. In conclusion, the paper posits that only democratically representative local governments, held accountable by empowered citizens and responsive to the needs and rights of local residents to participate in decision-making, can address the growing crisis in the Niger Delta.

Cyril Obi
Senior Researcher
The Nordic Africa Institute

Acknowledgement

The author is extremely grateful to the anonymous reviewers for their invaluable comments that have helped to shape the paper. Of course, the author accepts full responsibility for any inadequacies in this paper.

Introduction

What passes for federalism in Nigeria is more of a centralised political pact among state elites pursuing their common interests, including controlling and sharing power and resources, without paying much attention to the concerns of the governed. One possible explanation for this trend is federal control of oil revenues, which are in turn reallocated to the other tiers of government, namely state and local governments. Such resources are controlled either through interventionist/public agencies appointed by the federal government or through regional elites at various state levels, often without any real connections with local communities and peoples.

The federal government's response to the agitation in the Niger Delta for the control of resources has so far fallen short of satisfying the demands put forward by most groups in the oil-rich but impoverished region.[1] A fundamental shortcoming is that local people are not sufficiently involved in making decisions affecting them. This much has been recognised by officials of the federal government, who have noted that a deliberate policy should be adopted to 'get the Niger Delta people actively involved in defining their own development' (Obi 2008). A crucial challenge in this regard lies in the means by which the active participation of the Niger Delta people in their own governance can be secured. This challenge calls for local governance based on popular participation as a catalyst for local development and peace in the Niger Delta.[2]

Local government councils, which are constitutionally recognised as the third tier of government in Nigeria, come to mind as suitable loci for enhanced local participation in governance. Despite their constitutional role and immense potential in terms of grassroots politics and development, local governments have been largely overlooked in the literature on the Niger Delta conflict. This is in spite of the fact that they have 'a fundamentally important role in providing for basic social and economic rights' (Human Rights Watch 2007a). Entitled to a percentage of revenue allocation from federal and state governments (and also mandated to raise revenues through local taxes, levies and fees) and constitutionally assigned certain basic governmental responsibilities, local governments are definitely the level of government closest to the people of the Niger Delta. However, the local government system in Nigeria, especially in the Niger Delta, has so far operated largely as an extension of elite-dominated state politics, built

---

1.   Obi (2008) for instance argues that the struggle for resource control is directed at a return to 'the principles of true federalism', which demands a renegotiation of the structure of the Nigerian federation.

2.   The connection between the concept of federalism and the idea of local governance is one that requires more detailed interrogation. An attempt is made to engage this connection in the conceptual section of this work.

around networks of local patronage involving accumulation, cooption and distribution of largesse to support groups, including violent militias, contrary to
the ideal role of institutions for grassroots governance.

This paper critically examines local governance in the Niger Delta and its
relevance to the search for an inclusive and sustainable resolution of the conflict
in the oil-rich Niger Delta region. It also critiques the existing local government
system and explores the possible reconceptualising of local governance along
more inclusive, democratic, accountable and participatory forms that would in-
stitutionalise democracy, development and peace at the grassroots level. In addressing the challenge of grassroots democratic participation and social justice,
this paper provides insights into how local people perceive and relate to local
governments in the Niger Delta. The approach adopted in the paper is based
on a combination of methods and perspectives drawn from law and the social
sciences. It includes administering open-ended questions to 70 respondents in
three different local government areas across three states in the Niger Delta,
and the application of socio-legal methods of investigation and analysis. Consequently, the paper does not strictly conform to the conventional analytical forms
that most social scientists are familiar with.[3]

Considering the constitutionally stipulated structure of governance in Nigeria, local governments in the Niger Delta ought to be the primary political
structures for addressing the concerns and socioeconomic demands of peoples
at the grassroots. Either as an outlet for local people to articulate grievances or
as a channel for governmental responses to local demands, the local government system has the potential to promote peace and sustainable development.
However, systematic neglect by higher levels of government and the ineptitude
of local government officials, among other factors, have contributed to making
this level of governance ineffective.

The paper is organised in five sections, including the introduction. The second section makes some conceptual clarifications regarding local governance in
the Niger Delta. The third and fourth sections analyse the nature of local governance in the Niger Delta and its response to the crisis in the region. The fifth
and concluding section focuses on structural and democratic issues associated
with local governance in the Niger Delta. It also makes recommendations for
reinventing local governance for sustainable democratic grassroots development
in the region.

---

3. Questionnaires with open-ended questions were administered to 108 respondents spread
    across three states in the Niger Delta. Seventy of the respondents were based in Yenagoa in
    the Yenagoa Local Government Area of Bayelsa State, and 19 respondents each were based
    in Ahoada in the Ahoada Local Government Area of Rivers State and Patani in the Patani
    Local Government Area of Delta State. The respondents were from different walks of life
    and included civil servants, lawyers, graduate and undergraduate students, lecturers, a sec-
    ondary school teacher, two unemployed and one motor-cycle taxi operator.

Conceptual section: Local governance in a federal context

Local governance can be described as the 'working local systems of collective action that manage a locality's public affairs (on the basis of decentralisation) and are accountable to local residents' (Olowu and Wunsch 2004). In some ways, local governance is understood as one of several aspects of decentralisation (Olsen 2007). Increasingly, decentralisation has become a feature of governance structures in the developing world. Based on the idea of decentralisation, governments in the developing world are seen to be progressively 'transferring management responsibilities and powers from central government to a variety of local institutions' (Ribot 2003).

In fact, the view has been expressed that decentralisation has gained the status of 'one of the core components of political conditionality in international development cooperation' (Beall 2004). In other words, from Beall's point of view, developing states are compelled by development partners to adopt some form of decentralised governance structure, even where regimes in the developing states are not fully convinced that decentralisation is necessary. This suggests a developmental good imposed by external forces on unwilling developing states and the fact remains that decentralised local governance is not always accepted by everyone as a good thing. Secondly, it is certainly not alien to Africa.

The concept of local governance needs to be understood in more specific terms. According to one view, 'local governance is … the formulation and execution of collective action at the local level' (Shah and Shah 2006). Consequently, local governance 'encompasses the direct and indirect roles of formal institutions of local government and government hierarchies, as well as the roles of informal norms, networks, community organisations and neighbourhood associations in pursuing collective action by defining … interactions, collective decisions and delivery of local public services' (Shah and Shah 2006). Perhaps one of the more popular definitions of local governance is that used by the United Nations Development Programme (UNDP). According to the UNDP:

> Local governance comprises a set of institutions, mechanisms and processes through which citizens and their groups can articulate their interests and needs, mediate their differences, and exercise their rights and obligations at the local level. The building blocks of good local governance are many: citizen participation, partnerships among key actors at the local level, capacity of local actors across all sectors, multiple flows of information, institutions of accountability, and a pro-poor orientation. (UNDP 2004)

Clearly, both views of local governance go beyond mere structures of local government. In fact, as earlier commentators have observed from their analysis of the UNDP definition, the hallmark of local governance in its modern sense is stakeholder participation, more especially 'the involvement of the private sector and civil society in … interaction with governmental structures' (Olsen 2007). Viewed from this perspective, it is the processes rather than the constitutional/ legal structures that matter most, even though the legal framework remains crucial to the building of local governance. In fact, it is argued that 'good local governance is about … creating space for democratic participation and civic dialogue, supporting market-led and environmentally sustainable local development and facilitating outcomes that enrich the quality of life of residents' (Shah and Shah 2006: 2).

According to Stigler (1957), 'decision making should occur at the lowest level of government' as this is 'consistent with the goal of allocation efficiency' (Shah and Shah 2006). Two principles are adduced for this position. First, it is argued that 'the closer a representative government is to the people, the better it works.' Second, 'people should have the right to vote for the kind and amount of public services they want' (Stigler 1957). Taking the theory further, the correspondence principle as developed by Oates (1972) posits that 'the jurisdiction that determines the level of provision of each public good should include precisely the set of individuals who consume the goods' (cited by Shah and Shah 2006). Oates's decentralisation theorem (Oates 1972) posits further that 'each public service should be provided by the jurisdiction having control over the minimum geographic area that would internalize the benefits and costs of such provisions.'

Basically, there appears to be some agreement that government should be close enough to the people in order to create space for the active participation by those people. If this theoretical position is correct (as I suppose it is), it triggers the argument that in a federal state such as Nigeria, the lowest tier of government has more potential to ensure good local governance. In fact, some have made the point that the relationship between citizens in a given locality and local government institutions, which is what local democratic governance is about, is 'shaped by the federal structure of a nation's government' (Frey and Stutzer 2004). Arguably, the role that ordinary people would have to play in the governance process can best occur at the level closest to them. Federalism as a form of political arrangement in which some level of autonomy is exercised at the lowest level of government holds the promise for the kind of close interaction between people on the one hand and the structures and processes of local government on the other.

In light of the foregoing, it is safe to posit that the management of local affairs occurs at different levels of public and private governance. The point of departure for this paper is that the failure of local governance plays a major role in creating the popular frustration that underpins local resistance and consequently promotes violent conflict in the Niger Delta.

Generally, local governance in a multiethnic federal context would involve the devolution of specific powers and resources to the grassroots or community level. Such decentralisation involves empowering lower levels of government to exercise certain powers and serve local functions, including the provision of social services within a sphere of autonomy legally shielded from the supremacy of the central government. It also envisages the devolution of political, administrative and economic authority to lower levels of government with the aim of empowering local people to make decisions relevant to efficiency and effectiveness in the generation and management of resources (Hatchard et al. 2004: 184). In this sense, the existence of local government is justified by the fact that it creates opportunity for political participation, helps to ensure efficient service-delivery and consolidates opposition to the overbearing centralisation of governmental powers and functions (King and Stoker 1996: 6; Beall 2004). These features generally ought to enhance the interaction that good local governance envisages. Thus, in order to be effective as avenues for popular local participation, local governments need to be representative, accountable and responsive (Beetham 1996: 32).

In order to satisfy the element of representativeness, local government officials need to emerge from a transparent electoral process that ensures the enthronement of the choice of the majority. A transparent and functional electoral process provides a basis for the legitimacy of elected local government officials and their accountability to the populace. In this regard, elected officials are expected to implement priority programmes and projects for the benefit of the populace. It is also expected that they use public resources in a transparent manner and render accounts of the use of such resources and their stewardship to the local electorate. An important aspect of local governance relates to the need for local people to have access to, and exercise their right to demand information about the activities of local government officials, and hold them accountable for policies and actions undertaken in the course of their representation in government (Beetham 1996: 31).

Responsiveness is also vital for local governance to engender sustainable development. The latter requires local governments to 'take note systematically of the full range of public opinion in the formulation and implementation of law and policy' (Beetham 1996: 32). Hence, the responsiveness of local government is measured by its capacity to adopt policies that are demonstrably preferred by local people. Such demonstration of preference will be determined by a variety of procedures, including opinion polls and consultative forums which local people can claim as a matter of right (Przeworski et al. 1999: 9; Beetham 1996: 32). Generally, civil society ought also to play a significant role in the location of popular preferences. To meet the criteria for effectiveness, local governments require sufficient legal and actual (political) latitude and resources to exercise decision-making authority. This normally excludes unnecessary interference and overbearing involvement by higher levels of government in the processes and procedures of local governments (Greffe 2005: 47). The fundamental question that arises is whether local governance in the Niger Delta region of Nigeria satisfies the foregoing criteria. If it does not, then the prospects of its acting as a sociopolitical institution and process of sociopolitical conflict prevention in the region become problematic.

The issues in the Niger Delta struggle

A critical reading of the Niger Delta struggle shows that its main thrust is to bring about a better quality of life through the responsible and socially equitable application of the revenues that accrue from oil and gas exploration and production in the area.[4] Iyayi has grouped the demands of the region into eight. These are: a call for true federalism; demand for resource control and institution of fair derivation formula in the allocation of federal revenue; demand for self-determination; demand for the restoration of the environment; demand for change in the legislative framework for oil and gas exploration; demand for infrastructures and social services; demand for an end to the war in the Niger Delta; and altering the neocolonial, dependent nature of the Nigerian state (Iyayi 2007). Iyayi's observation is seemingly reinforced by Obi, who sees the struggle as 'a collective action directed at blocking further alienation, expropriation and environmental degradation' (Obi 2008). As will be demonstrated shortly, some of these demands are not without structural and other complications, even for the region itself.

From an African human rights perspective, most of the demands fall within clear internationally protected rights, such as the right to the best attainable state of health, the right to existence and self-determination, the right of peoples to freely dispose of their wealth and natural resources, the right to development, the right to national and international peace and the right to a satisfactory environment (African Charter 1981: Arts 16, 20, 21, 22, 23, 24).[5]

However, the rights guaranteed in the African Charter on Human and Peoples' Rights have to be enjoyed in line with the fundamental principles of the Constitutive Act of the African Union (see, African Charter 1981: Art 56 section 2). Thus, to the extent that article 4(b) of the Constitutive Act of the African Union requires the Union to respect borders that existed at the time of

---

4. This wide term 'better quality of life' is intended to cover popular participation, compensation, environmental sustainability, employment and political inclusion.

5. In its landmark decision in *SERAC and Another v Nigeria* (2001), the African Commission on Human and Peoples Rights found Nigeria liable for the violation of some rights of the Ogoni people.

independence, the rights that arguably underlie the Niger Delta demands may only be achievable within the existing national boundaries of the political entity called Nigeria. Indeed, the African Commission on Human and Peoples' Rights (African Commission) has previously emphasised that even though the right to self-determination is recognised in the African Charter, it has to be enjoyed taking full cognisance of sovereignty and territorial integrity, which the African Commission saw itself as bound to uphold (*Katangese Peoples' Congress v Zaire* 2000). Consequently, the demand by the Niger Delta for self-determination is currently laden with legal complications. While this provision envisages consultation by government to identify the manner by which a group wishes to exercise self-determination, it also gives the state a right to protect colonial territorial boundaries.

It is against this background that the call for true federalism stands out as the most reasonable, attractive and achievable demand in the context of the Niger Delta. In Iyayi's view, the demand for true federalism envisages 'the autonomy and initiative' of the states *vis-à-vis* the central government. It also contemplates the right of the states in the region to take responsibility for security through the establishment of their own police forces and the decentralisation of governance through the right to create local governments (Iyayi 2007).[6] This would coincide with the theoretical perspective that authentic decentralisation of governance presupposes 'downwardly accountable or representative authorities with meaningful discretionary powers' that should lead to 'local efficiency, equity and development' (Ribot 2003: 53).

One element that sticks out in the demand for 'true federalism' as championed by the ruling class in the region is that the principle is to apply to the relationship between states and the federal government but not to any relationship between states and local governments and communities. In essence, there seems to be a parting of ways in the struggle to the extent that the expectations of militants and would-be militants reach down to control of resources by local people through community foundations (International Crisis Group 2006). More importantly, the expectations of communities appear to correspond with the expectations of the militants rather than those of the elite groups.[7] Linked

---

6. Under the existing federal arrangement, states do not have powers to establish their own police forces. States however, do have the right to initiate the creation of local government in collaboration with the federal government acting through the National Assembly (see, 1999 Constitution of Nigeria: section 8(3)). Despite this provision, the federal government under former President Obasanjo resisted the creation of new local government councils in places like Bayelsa State in the Niger Delta region.

7. About 95% of respondents to a questionnaire developed to gauge the feeling of people in Bayelsa State and Delta State hold the view that decentralisation should occur as between states and local government councils. A modest 108 people responded to the questionnaire. Result on file with this author.

to this is the introduction of the concept of community-specific grievance that is explained as dissatisfaction with the state of development of individual communities as distinct from the states and the region. Such community grievances, it is contended, also create motivation for armed struggle (Oyefusi 2008).

At this level, local resistance to the federal government (and oil companies) is championed by different groups, while the state governments in the Niger Delta are largely ignored, partly because they are perceived as conduits for the limited distribution of wealth. Essentially, local governments, community development authorities and youth organisations participate only to the extent they serve as forums for dialogue (or more appropriately, channels by which information is handed down by state officials). Armed groups, for their part, engage the coercive apparatus of the federal government in their demand for redistribution of petroleum wealth in favour of local communities. Against this background, it is possible to perceive a gap in local governance in the region.

With respect to the intervention agencies set up by the Nigerian state, some hold the view that these institutions were positive measures. Ebeku argues that 'from a close view, it seems the Oil Mineral Producing Areas Development Commission (OMPADEC) had laudable objectives …' (Ebeku 2006). Suberu (1996:39) 'believes that OMPADEC recorded "impressive achievements"'. However a deeper examination reveals that the interventionist agencies have been useful vehicles for creating wealth for a certain class of citizens in the Niger Delta region. It is those who are privileged enough to be 'connected' to decision-makers in the interventionist agencies that have the opportunity to accumulate vast amounts of wealth through the award of contracts.[8] Thus, it is not uncommon to find local citizens who have been 'empowered' financially through contracts with these agencies. It is also the case that certain basic facilities, such as low-cost roads, water boreholes and landing jetties, which have failed to be delivered to certain local communities through the conventional apparatus of state government, have been brought to such communities by interventionist agencies. Naturally, local people without any other hope of such facilities, especially in the face of ignorance regarding the responsibilities of government, tend to view such interventions by the agencies with complete gratitude. However, one of the most important roles played by these agencies is the provision of a platform for collaboration between the various tiers of government and major stakeholders in the oil industry, particularly multinational oil companies. This role is one that the agencies are better suited to perform than local governments.

Despite the isolated reports of positive contributions to the development of the region, the overwhelming evidence suggests that these agencies have not

---

8. Informal interviews with a limited number of respondents who prefer to be anonymous.

been very successful.[9] As far back as August 2008, governors of the Niger Delta states admitted to the failure of projects initiated by state governments and the intervention agencies of the federal government, including the Niger Delta Development Commission (NDDC) (*Vanguard Newspapers* 2008). The interventionist institutions of state governments have also received mixed appraisals, though the overwhelming view appears to be that interventions by these agencies do not justify the huge sums allocated to them.[10] One of the biggest failures of the interventionist agencies is that they mostly give rise to elitist projects, creating patron-client networks to the detriment of the wider sections of local communities. The interventionist agencies have also been unable to address some of the biggest challenges facing communities. This is partly due to the withholding of funds owing to these agencies by the government. The situation is further worsened by allegations of massive corruption among leading figures in the management and boards of these agencies.

Despite the damning assessments, interventionist institutions are perceived by some locals to have fared better than local governments in terms of their impact on the lives of ordinary people. Evidence of this perception can be found in the fact that local people, especially chiefs and local elites, have no difficulty in defending the continued existence of these agencies.[11] This perception is arguably fuelled by the fact that interventionist agencies have been able to fund apparently conspicuous projects in different parts of the region that local governments have hitherto been unable to fund. The point must be made that the perception needs further interrogation, as there is as yet no study analysing local government performance *vis-à-vis* resources available to these levels of government.

The superior performance of interventionist agencies can be partly explained by the fact that local governments receive far less funding from the federal revenue purse.[12] For example, out of 5.446 trillion naira distributed from the federal account in 2008, the 774 local government councils together got only 1.051

---

9. Most respondents in interviews conducted by this author in the course of research for this paper took the view that only 'sycophants and people who benefit from contracts awarded by OMPADEC and NDDC can claim that these bodies are useful to the region' (on file with author).

10. Generally, state governments allocated between 40% and 50% of the 13% derivation that accrues to them from state interventionist agencies.

11. In the research for this contribution, all respondents to informal interviews claimed that the agencies were the only way that the region gets a part of what is due to it.

12. Whereas the NDDC, for instance, receives contributions from the 13% derivation fund and oil companies, the oil-producing area commissions of the states receive their funding from the derivation revenue that accrues to the given state. Local governments, for their part, only receive funding from the federal allocation, part of which is deducted by the various state governments. With very little tax base, local government councils face an uphill task in terms of generating funds.

trillion naira.[13] In any event, the impact of the agencies arises from the fact that elites get awarded contracts that put money in their pockets, while the people benefit from shabbily executed road and water projects that do not last for very long. Furthermore, in terms of the engagement of civil society as a major component of local governance, the agencies fare better as there is hardly any constructive involvement of civil society in the processes of local government administration. This is different from the situation with some interventionist agencies, where some effort is made to engage with civil society and community-based groups. It is essential to point out that there is some fallacy in comparing the performance and quality of governance of local government councils and interventionist agencies, since they are not substitutes for one another. Yet in the Nigerian context, interventionist agencies commonly try to duplicate the functions and responsibilities of different tiers of government.

Discussions with grassroots people in Niger Delta society suggest the widespread perception of state and federal politicians as elites that feed off oil resources that could be better utilised for local development purposes. Linked to this perception is the image in the minds of local citizens and residents that the power relations in the polity as reinforced by the prevailing legal regime protect the elite from accountability to the public (see, Federal Republic of Nigeria 1999: Section 308).[14] It is also obvious that complaints of marginalisation at the federal level on the grounds of the (ethnic) minority status of the Niger Delta people are equally relevant at the state level, where certain ethnic groups or communities are smaller in size and constitute micro minorities.[15] This implies that minority groups that suffer 'double' marginalisation within the Niger Delta states can only find a measure of succour if they have their own units of local representation and governance.

Local governance in the Niger Delta: The challenge of democracy and development

The challenge that the communities and peoples of the Niger Delta face is as much about the need for development as it is about self-determination. Development relates essentially to the question of governance (Iyayi 2007: 26; Hatchard et al. 2004). The developmental challenge in the region is linked to the democratic deficit in the polity. Since local people have little or no say in the choice of lead-

---

13. See report at http://www.fmf.gov.ng/downloads/faacsummary2008.pdf
14. This section gives immunity to the President, Vice President, Governors and Deputy Governors and is an example of such laws.
15. In this regard, it is difficult to imagine the Epie people in Bayelsa State having a strong position in relation to the larger Izon group in the distribution of state revenue.

ers and no control over the management of resources, the existing governmental configuration fails to address the developmental needs of the communities.[16]

The current political structures and power relations in the Niger Delta ensure that local government elections are manipulated/hijacked by the incumbent ruling party (International Crisis Group 2006). Consistently, the party in power in each state has won all local government elections in polls conducted by electoral bodies appointed by the same party in power and characterised by extremely low voter turnouts. Under such conditions, elections fail to meet the minimum standards in municipal constitutions and as agreed upon by African states in several regional and continental instruments. Thus, those that end up being elected in the flawed elections to run local governments are not true representatives of the people, nor do they consider themselves as being accountable to the electorate, as they owe their positions to powerful political godfathers within the ruling party. As such, the oil revenues that trickle down to the local level invariably end up in private pockets of politically powerful and connected individuals or used to lubricate patron-client networks linked to those in control of power at the state level.

The subversion of the democratic will of the people of the Niger Delta has resulted in citizens leading a degraded life of poverty and underdevelopment laced with severe insecurity. From the African human rights law perspective, the inability of the Nigerian state to ensure effective service delivery for the benefit of its citizens violates treaty obligations under the African Charter in areas such as the right to life, right to dignity, the right to the best attainable state of physical and mental health and the right to education (African Charter 1981: Arts 4, 5, 16, 17). There is also a clear violation of the rights to participation and self-determination, as guaranteed under the African Charter. This is important, since in the absence of a right to secede, quality local governance in an autonomous and transparent process becomes the option available to local people, such as the citizens of the Niger Delta.

Ideally, local governance in Nigeria should be carried out by decentralising the apparatus of government. Decentralisation of government in Nigeria dates back to colonial times, but it was only in 1976 that local government was formally and statutorily recognised as the third tier of government in Nigeria (Olowu and Wunsch 2004). Multiplying in numbers as a result of state and local government creation activities by military juntas over the years, there are currently 774 local government area councils listed in the 1999 Constitution of

---

16. The damning reports of election observers and monitors over the last few elections are an indication of this deficit.

Nigeria.[17] Of these, 185 were created for states in the 'political Niger Delta' region.[18] The constitution requires local government councils to be democratically administered and imposes a constitutional duty on states to ensure the existence of democratically elected local councils under state law, subject to constitutional guidelines (Federal Republic of Nigeria 1999: Section 7).[19] Accordingly, while local governments are constitutional creations, they operate under the local government laws of the various states. They are administered by executive chairmen and local councils subject to the supervision of a commissioner and auditor-general in each state.

As with all other local government councils in Nigeria, the functions and powers of local government councils in the Niger Delta are spelt out in the constitution and in the local government laws of the various states, in this case the Niger Delta states. In addition to responsibility for minor service delivery in areas such as collection of rates and licences, construction and maintenance of cemeteries, destitute homes, roads, streets, drains and other enumerated items, local governments are expected to participate in the governance of states, especially in the provision and maintenance of basic education and health services. To finance their projects, local governments are authorised to raise funds from the collection of rates and issuance of licences to complement statutory allocations from federal and state governments. Under the state laws, these powers and functions of local government are statutorily required to be performed by democratically elected officials. At face value, decentralisation operates on globally acceptable criteria and local governments should enhance development of local communities through constructive local governance. However, both in legal structure and in actual operation, especially in view of the financial starvation that they face, local governments in Nigeria are seemingly designed to fail in their administrative functioning and in service delivery. Hence, as indicated in the Human Rights Watch Report (2007: 24–5), local governments in the Niger Delta spend the greater percentage of their allocations to pay salaries. This reality continues.

Damning reports from international organisations are not the only records

---

17. With the implementation of the judgment of the International Court of Justice affirming Cameroon's ownership of the Bakassi area, leading to Nigeria's ceding of the Bakassi Local Government Area of Cross Rivers State to Cameroon, 773 of the constitutionally recognised local government areas remain. There has also been a spate of inchoate local government area creations in some states, but these have failed to receive formal recognition by the federal government.

18. In the Nigerian political context, all states in which petroleum resources are found are generally classified as part of the Niger Delta, even though some of them do not fall within the geographical area of the Niger Delta.

19. See sec 7 of the 1999 Constitution of Nigeria.

of the failure of existing local government structures in the Niger Delta. Among most people in the region, the perception of local governance is very negative. In response to structured questionnaires, 102 out of 108 respondents opined that local government councils in the region do not live up to expectations.[20] In fact, apart from respondents who referred to the 1999 Constitution before answering, when asked what the functions of local government authorities are, most respondents were not very sure, mostly because they claimed not to have experienced any impact of local governance. Confronted with the statement of functions in the constitution and in the local government laws, the common response was that no local government council performs more than 10 per cent of its statutory functions. Naturally, the general view expressed by respondents was that in their current form, local governments in the Niger Delta cannot improve the lives of people in the region.[21]

Structural challenges in the local government system can be found in constitutional ambiguities regarding the delineation of functions between states and local governments (Khemani 2004). The itemisation of relatively insignificant functions for local governments and creation of a mere participatory role in more significant areas while granting states complete authority in those areas results in a lack of clarity about what communities can expect of local governments in the Niger Delta. In addition to the constitutional entrenchment of state control over local government administration, provision is made for states to relieve local authorities of all but the most unimportant duties, such as payment of staff salaries and maintenance of markets in order to limit the need for greater allocation of revenue to local government. Furthermore, the existing legal regime severely restricts the ability of local governments to raise revenue internally. In essence, local governments emerge as ineffective and undeserving of further revenue allocation. At the same time, opportunity is created for inadequate funding to be used as a justification for non-performance, allowing for relaxation of control and thus leaving greater scope for corruption at this level of government.[22]

With no significant governmental functions to carry out, local governments in the Niger Delta, as in most other parts of the country, are seen as irrelevant to grassroots development. One possible effect of this is that no matter how much revenue flows to local coffers, local governments still fail to provide even the

---

20. Informal interviews/poll conducted by this author in March 2011 in which 108 respondents from Bayelsa and Delta states participated. Results on file with the author.

21. It is recognised that the analysis of the data from the responses does not strictly comply with the standards of social science as a discipline. However, the focus is on the overall picture to demonstrate the challenges of local governance in the region rather than to create pin-point accuracy in data collection and evaluation.

22. Under current revenue allocation formula, local government councils share approximately 18% of the total revenue that accrues to the federation account.

most basic services to local communities. This reinforces the feeling of neglect. More dangerously, local people fail to identify the link between governance deficit at the local level and lack of development in the region, hence losing the opportunity to take control of the management of the limited resources that accrue to them. Civil society, which ought to demand better services and accountability, is all but non-existent in local government in the region. Local officials themselves inadvertently contribute to this negative perception by exhibiting a lack of transparency in the fiscal operations of local councils. This comes out very strongly in the budgeting process of local government councils. For instance, over a period of three years it has proven almost impossible to access the budgets of any local government council in Bayelsa and Delta states. Such difficulties confront individuals just as much as they confront corporate bodies.[23] This has led one organisation to conclude that 'in most of the local governments, budget documents were simply not available as councils do not work with budgets' (NDCBP 2009: 6).

In terms of democratic requirements, local government, which ought to be the building block for nurturing a national democratic culture of mass political participation, currently leaves so much to be desired. Generally, political participation by local people should be greater at local government levels, where people can vote for council officials personally known to them, thereby achieving direct local control over governance and local resources. However, it is not uncommon for state governors in the Niger Delta to appoint caretaker committees to administer local governments.[24] They often appoint the party faithful and cronies to such committees, thereby controlling local governments and removing any chance of accountability by local officials to the people.

Thus, the democratic principle of using elections to enhance accountability is absent and local governance is deprived of any form of accountability. Even where local government elections are conducted, in most cases violence and massive electoral fraud ensure that the results do not represent the will of the people (Human Rights Watch 2005). The 2004 local government elections in Rivers State, for instance, were riddled with allegations of massive rigging and violence. This is largely the trend in nearly all other states in the Niger Delta. Local officials emerging from such processes lack legitimacy and often the motivation to respond to the needs of local communities, thus defeating the

---

23. This author tried and failed to access any budget even though the author is indigenous to the Niger Delta region. Corporate institutions such as Human Rights Watch could only access budgets from five out of 23 local government areas in Rivers State for its 2006 report. Similarly, the Niger Delta Citizen Budget Platform was unable to get responses from both states and local governments when the Platform formally requested budget documents for its 2009 budget monitoring project.
24. As at January 2009, local government councils in Bayelsa State were being administered by caretaker committees.

representative aspect of local governance. In fact, local people face the 'danger of local elite capture of democratised local governments' (Crook and Sverrisson 1999: 3). Hence, as presently constituted local government councils in the Niger Delta arguably lack the democratic legitimacy to facilitate development in the region.

As noted earlier, accountability in the prioritisation of projects and management of local resources is an essential aspect of local governance for sustainable development. Ordinarily, local government laws in force in the Niger Delta states recognise the need for accountability by requiring council chairmen to submit annual budgets to local councillors and vesting authority in the councils to control withdrawals from local government accounts (Bayelsa State Local Government Law 2000: Section 40).[25] This is in addition to making local government secretaries and treasurers the signatories to local government accounts and empowering local government inspectors to inspect local government accounts. The requirement of annual budgets should give local people control through their elected representatives to determine the projects to which funds are allocated and monitor the use of such funds. However, in practice, annual budgets are currently perceived as formalities with no real impact on the accountability of local officials (Human Rights Watch 2006).

In terms of the case for greater allocation of resources to local governments, the inflow of revenue to that level appears to have improved in recent years. However, the accountability of local officials does not seem to have improved because as earlier studies have shown, 'local capture' has replaced state and federal-level corruption (Wantchekon and Asadurian 2002). Local governments are seen as avenues for local politicians to generate instant wealth for themselves and their protégés. Some commentators have linked the problem of accountability to lack of access to information by local people regarding the allocation of revenues to lower levels from higher levels of government, and the resultant apathy, since councils do not depend on taxes paid by the people themselves (Khemani 2004).

This arguably indicates the limitations of civil society in addressing the local governance deficits in the region. With little or no expectation of service delivery among local people, demand for accountability is lowered and local public executives are at liberty to embezzle local government funds.[26] This situation enables states to justify reduction of funds accruable to the local governments and makes local governments unsuitable drivers of sustainable development.

---

25. Printed by the Bayelsa State Government Printer.
26. Human Rights Watch reports that in some local government areas in Rivers State, chairmen are known to have allocated funds in their budgets for projects being undertaken by other levels of government. Personal interviews conducted by this author also showed that local chairmen were usually only expected to allocate wages and salaries, leaving large sums of money to be 'shared' amongst local politicians.

Regrettably, despite the widespread allegations of corruption in local government councils, there is often no hard evidence to sustain a trial, not to mention a conviction. This trend reflects the challenges of fighting corruption at the federal and state levels where, despite common knowledge of widespread abuse of office and mismanagement of funds, anti-corruption agencies are frustrated in their bids to ensure convictions.

Closely linked to the accountability challenge facing local governments in the Niger Delta is the question of responsiveness. Considering the proximity of local governments to local communities, they ought to be able to gauge local feelings and respond to the main local needs quicker than other levels of government. The expectation in various local government laws is that councillors representing wards comprising relatively few people should serve as links between local government and their people. There is almost no recognition of a role for civil society and there is hardly any activity in that sector. However, despite the expectations regarding councillors, there is either a 'disconnect' between local councils and the people or there is collusion between councillors and local government chairmen, allowing for speedy approval of budgets without proper scrutiny or reference to community needs.

In extreme cases (which are becoming more common), councillors are unable to appreciate the dynamics of budgeting, and budgets from previous years are reportedly simply transferred to the next. This is fuelled by the fact that in most local government areas in the region aspirants to council office are very often holders of primary school leaving certificates, with absolutely no training in or capacity for budgeting. It is also common to find local governments in the Niger Delta prioritising irrelevant projects in the face of more pressing needs of the communities. For example, in one local government area funds were allocated to build a football academy, a project unconnected to the needs of the local communities (Human Rights Watch 2007a).

Another very common practice in local government councils in the Niger Delta is the construction of new council buildings by new administrations. In the Patani Local Government Area of Delta State the new council building structures have remained unused several years after they were built. In remoter areas, local officials are notorious for staying away from local government headquarters until it is time to collect monthly allocations.[27] In these circumstances, local governments contradict claims to responsiveness to the needs of local communities. With such apparent failures of governance at the level closest to local people, feelings of neglect and dissatisfaction are reinforced, creating a condu-

---

27. Respondents interviewed from areas like Ekeremor Local Government Area in Bayelsa State and Bomadi Local Government Area in Delta State alluded to this trend.

cive environment for the ventilation of frustration by alternative means such as armed local resistance.

The conclusion from this analysis is that there is a democratic deficit in local governance in the Niger Delta. Local government chairmen have been described as people with 'no goals, no objectives, nothing they want to accomplish'. Rather, 'ninety-nine per cent think of local government as nothing more than an opportunity to get paid for doing nothing' (Human Rights Watch 2007b).[28] This conclusion supports the observation of one auditor-general for local government who saw a need to 'restore sanity to the state's local governments' (Human Rights Watch 2006). Some observers argue that local government administration in the region suffers from a shortage of skilled manpower to run local affairs (interview with Thankgod Ogbomah).[29] Several local respondents also saw a need to 'revamp the system and make local governments more accountable'. Yet, these same local governments produce the officials that manage public affairs at state and federal levels. Others blame gaps in the mechanism for accountability and the high rate of corruption at the local level (interview with anonymous respondent).[30]

Notwithstanding the foregoing, the prospects for accountability are arguably better at the local level than at higher levels of government. With no immunity, no control of state instruments of coercion and with greater accessibility to local people, it is easier for the management of resources to be effectively monitored at the local level. The local government level is also better positioned for the mobilization of civil society to monitor resource allocations.

Conclusion: The challenge of reinventing local democratic governance in the Niger Delta

In the face of obvious governance challenges, local government administration in the Niger Delta needs to be reinvented. A starting point would be revisiting the constitutional provisions for local government in Nigeria. While it is true that some of the more efficient and effective local government systems in the world are not built only on the basis of constitutional entrenchment (Steytler 2005), it has to be noted that in its infancy local governance in Nigeria requires firm constitutional enthronement to be effective. In this regard, a constitutional review of the local government system is essential for revamping the operation of local government authorities in the Niger Delta.

---

28. Observations of the head of a local NGO in Port Harcourt, Rivers State.
29. Thankgod Ogbomah is a Yenagoa-based legal practitioner.
30. Interview with a former local government chairman and current member of the Bayelsa State Local Government Service Commission, who prefers to be anonymous.

Despite the focus on local governance in the Niger Delta, the challenges of local governance arguably apply to the entire Nigerian local government system. Thus, a very common perception is that local government councils constitute the weakest tier of governance in Nigeria. However, in the context of armed conflict in the Niger Delta and the root causes of local resistance, the need for reform in the region is greater. As local government councils have no role in collecting or distributing petroleum revenue, the efficacy potential of local governance may not be immediately obvious. Yet, since mismanagement of resources is a major part of the governance challenge that has led to armed local resistance, the relevance of reinventing local governance for peace and development cannot be overemphasised.

Despite the seemingly complex nature that armed local resistance has taken in the region, the fact remains that armed groups rely heavily on the support of local communities to sustain their operations. This is exhibited in the willingness of local communities to 'host' militant camps and their refusal to expose known militants. Thus, revamping the local government system to give local people a greater say in and control of resources would serve as an incentive for local communities to sever links with and discontinue support for armed groups. It would also give local communities a legitimate democratic platform to secure better access to oil revenue. Clearly, this approach envisages a major shake-up of the entire national political system, but it can start at the most basic and local level.

The reinvention of local governance in the Niger Delta has to involve a radical democratisation of local government administration in ways that facilitate greater participation of local people in governance. In relation to the representative character of local governance, the screening process for election into the leadership of local government offices has to be revised to encourage participation by the true representatives of the people. Local communities should be allowed to freely choose their representatives without the burden of partisan politics.[31] Massive grassroots reorientation is also necessary to educate local people on the value of their votes as mechanisms of ensuring representation, accountability and transparency by elected local officials. It is in this way that committed and skilled administrators with the legitimacy arising from a popular mandate can emerge to occupy the political space currently being contested by un-mandated (self-serving) militants and unrepresentative local government officials.

More crucial is the need to enhance actual empowerment of and participation by local residents in the decision-making processes of local government councils. While the difficulties linked with involving the general public in mak-

31. The fact that nearly all communities conduct 'credible' elections for community bodies such as community development committees is testimony to their success in managing their own affairs if there is no external interference.

ing technical decisions are acknowledged, it is increasingly recognised that local residents need to be actively involved in identifying projects and programmes requiring priority attention in the communities and regions. Examples of popular participation in local governance from other parts of the world include widespread consultations, public hearings, townhall meetings and participation in consumer societies targeting local government projects (Bucek and Smith 2000: 4). Referendums are also common in enhancing local involvement in decision-making. Taking into account the technicalities and costs associated with some of these mechanisms, but also conscious of the need to ensure that residents of the region are empowered to take decisions that reflect their interests and protect their dignity, it is recommended that innovations drawn from other parts of the world be studied and adapted to address the specific needs of the Niger Delta.

Along with the democratisation of local government and strengthening of the quality of local government personnel, there should be willingness to empower local governments in the region with greater responsibilities and functions. Under the present regime in most Niger Delta states, vertical oversight functions are performed by ministries or bureaus of local government, auditors-general of local government, state assemblies and, in some cases, by local government inspectors. Horizontal oversight is usually done by local government councillors. However, these institutions have not been effective because, more often than not, all these layers of oversight are manned by members of the political party controlling the state government. This creates a sense of common destiny and self-preservation among councillors, thereby resulting in half-hearted supervision.

To strengthen existing modes of accountability in governance, citizen control needs to be introduced with options such as independent legal action against misappropriation and community verification and supervision of entrenched projects.[32] It would not be out of place to also require outgoing local government officials to submit to judicial or quasi-judicial scrutiny at the end of their tenures with the aim of securing a certificate of fitness for public office following such a scrutiny. Over and above all these, a sense of community ownership of local government revenue has to be created to enable citizens to collectively protect the allocation and use of local funds. This is important because 'an alert and active citizen body' is vital for accountability (Beetham 1996: 33). In extreme cases, lack of ownership creates an exploitative view of local government revenue as resources to be exploited rather than protected (Ake 1995).

While traditional rulers currently have a limited advisory role in local governance, other important stakeholders such as community development com-

---

32. For instance, it is reported that in the Southern Ijaw Local Government Area of Bayelsa State, a citizens' forum independently set up a project committee to verify projects supposedly embarked upon by a local government administration.

mittees, local elite and armed groups have not been given any role. Although the undemocratic manner in which some of these stakeholders emerge creates difficulty for any argument in favour of giving them a significant role in governance, these actors can play important roles as checks on local and state officials. Also, civil society involvement in governance at the local level has to be prioritised if the responsiveness of local government is to be improved. This requires expansive civic education and the liberalisation of access to information regarding resource generation, allocation and use.

Local government councils need to be reconceptualised as agents for transformation of the 'petrolised' Niger Delta society. In this reconception, democratically transformed local government councils should be the context for addressing local grievances in the Niger Delta and should be acknowledged as a viable replacement for the none-too-successful interventionist agencies. It is suggested that resources currently administered by the interventionist agencies be transferred to empowered local government councils in order to give local people direct access to funds and a say in their allocation. It is, however, important that such transfer can only be effectively utilised if the structure and process of local governance is radically transformed. If they are not, then it should be pointed out that the current local governments in the region lack the capacity, will, leadership and legitimacy to transform the region.

This study has demonstrated that democratically representative local governments that are accountable and responsive to local needs are essential to addressing the growing crisis in the Niger Delta. This requirement does not displace the call for greater resource control or any of the other genuine claims of the region. Rather, it only complements the call for true federalism and emphasises the need to place the focus of governance and development at the level closest to local communities, instead of creating more wealth for centralisation and the mismanagement of resources in the oil-producing region.

References

African Charter on Human and Peoples Rights, 1982, *International Legal Materials* 21(8).

Ake, C., 1995, *Democracy and development in Africa*. Washington: Brookings Institution.

Bayelsa State Government, 2000, *Local Government Law 2000*. Cape Town: LexisNexis.

Beall, J, 2004, *Decentralisation and engendering democracy: Lessons from local government reform in South Africa*. Crisis States Research Centre Working Papers Series 1, 54. London: Crisis States Research Centre.

Beetham, D., 1996, "Theorising democracy and local government", in King, D. and G. Stoker (eds), *Rethinking Local Democracy*. London: Macmillan.

Brundlandt Commission Report (World Commission on Environment and Development), 1987. Oxford: Oxford University Press.

Bucek, J. and B. Smith, 2000, "New approaches to local democracy: Direct democracy, participation and the 'third sector'", *Environment and Planning C-Government and Policy* 18(1).

Crook, R.C., and A.S. Sverrisson, 1999, "To What Extent Can Decentralised Forms of Government Enhance the Development of Pro-Poor Policies and Improve Poverty-Alleviation Outcomes." Paper commissioned by UK Department of International Development, http://siteresources.worldbank.org/INTPOVERTY/Resources/WDR/DfiD-Project-Papers/crook.pdf (accessed on September 14, 2011).

Ebeku, K.S.A., 2006, *Oil and the Niger Delta People in International Law*. Cologne: Köppe Verlag.

Fagbadebo, O., 2007, "Corruption, governance and political instability in Nigeria", *African Journal of Political Science and International Relations* 1(2):28–37.

Federal Republic of Nigeria, 1982, *Allocation of Revenue (Federation Accounts) Act 2*. Lagos: Federal Government Press.

—, 1999, *Constitution of Nigeria in Laws of the Federation*. Lagos: Federal Government Press.

—, 1963, *Constitution of Nigeri.* Lagos: Federal Government Press.

Federal Republic of Nigeria, *Niger Delta Development Commission Act 2000* in *Laws of the Federation 200*. Cape Town: LexisNexis Butterworths.

Greffe X., S. Pflieger and A. Noya, 2005, *Culture and local development*. Paris: OECD.

Hatchard, J., M. Ndulo and P. Slinn, 2004, *Comparative constitutionalism and good governance in the Commonwealth*. Cambridge: Cambridge University Press.

Human Rights Watch, 2005, "Rivers and Blood: Guns, Oil and Power in Nigeria's Rivers State", Human Rights Watch Briefing Paper, February.

—, 2007a, "Chop Fine: The Human Rights Impact of Local Government Corruption and Mismanagement in Rivers State, Nigeria", *Human Rights Watch* 19(2a).

Ibeanu, O. and R. Luckman, 2006, *Niger Delta: Political Violence, Governance and Corporate Responsibility in a Petro-state*. Abuja: Centre for Democracy and Development (CDD).

International Crisis Group, 2006, "Nigeria: Want in the Midst of Plenty," Africa Report No. 113, 19 July, p. 7, http://www.crisisgroup.org/home/index.cfm?id=4274&l=1 (accessed August 7, 2011).

Iyayi, F., 2007, *The Niger Delta: Issues of Justice and Development Agenda*. Abuja: Centre for Democracy and Development.

Katangese Peoples' Congress v Zaire, 2000, AHRLR 72 (ACHPR 1995).

Khemani, S., 2004, "Local government accountability for service delivery in Nigeria" World Bank Research, Washington DC: The World Bank (available at http://siteresources.worldbank.org/INTPUBSERV/Resources/stuti_nigeria.pdf (accessed August 7, 2011).

King, D.S. and G. Stoker (eds), 1996, *Rethinking local democracy*. London: Macmillan.

Niger Delta Citizens and Budget Platform, 2009, "Beyond Amnesty – Citizens Report on State and Local Government Budgets in the Niger Delta".

Obi, C.I., 2006, *Youth and Generational Dimensions to the Struggles for Resource Control in the Niger Delta*. Dakar: CODESRIA.

—, 2008, "Enter the dragon? Chinese oil companies and resistance in the Niger Delta", *Review of African Political Economy* 35(117):417–34.

Okoh, R.N. and P.C. Egbon, 1999, Fiscal Federalism and Revenue Allocation: *The Poverty of the Niger Delta, in The Nigerian Economic Society*. Fiscal Federalism and Nigeria's Economic Development. Selected Papers Presented at the 1999 Annual Conference, Abuja, Nigeria, 405–20.

Olowu, D. and J.S. Wunsch, 2004, *Local Governance in Africa: The challenges of democratic decentralisation*. Boulder CO: Lynne Rienner.

Oyefusi. A., 2008, "Oil and the probability of rebel participation among youths in the Niger Delta of Nigeria", *Journal of Peace* 42:539.

Pernthaler, P. and A. Gamper, 2005, "Local government in Australia", in Steytler, N. (ed.), *The place and role of local government in a federal system*. Johannesburg: Konrad Adenauer Stiftung, Occasional Papers, November.

Przeworski A, S.C. Stokes and B. Manin, 1999, *Democracy, accountability and representation*. Cambridge: Cambridge University Press.

Ribot, J.C., 2003, "Democratic decentralisation of natural resources: Institutional choice and discretionary power transfers in sub-Saharan Africa", *Public Administration and Development* 23(1).

Shah, A. and S. Shah, 2006, "The new vision of local governance and the evolving roles of local governments" , in Shah. A., *Local Governance in Developing Countries*. Washington DC: The World Bank.

Social and Economic Rights Action Center (SERAC) and Another v Nigeria, 2001, AHRLR 60 (ACHPR 2001).

Steytler, N. (ed.), 2005, *The place and role of local government in a federal system.* Johannesburg: Konrad Adenauer Stiftung, Occasional Papers, November.

Vanguard Newspapers, 2008 (Nigeria), www.vanguardngr.com, August.

Wantchekon, L. and T. Asadurian, 2002, "Transfer Dependence and Regional Disparities: The Case of Nigeria". Center for Research on Economic Development and Policy Reform, Working Paper No. 152, August.

World Bank, 1989, *Sub-Saharan Africa from Crisis to Sustainable Development.* Washington: World Bank.

DISCUSSION PAPERS PUBLISHED BY THE INSTITUTE

Recent issues in the series are available electronically for download free of charge
www.nai.uu.se

1. Kenneth Hermele and Bertil Odén, *Sanctions and Dilemmas. Some Implications of Economic Sanctions against South Africa.* 1988. 43 pp. ISBN 91-7106-286-6

2. Elling Njål Tjönneland, *Pax Pretoriana. The Fall of Apartheid and the Politics of Regional Destabilisation.* 1989. 31 pp. ISBN 91-7106-292-0

3. Hans Gustafsson, Bertil Odén and Andreas Tegen, *South African Minerals. An Analysis of Western Dependence.* 1990. 47 pp. ISBN 91-7106-307-2

4. Bertil Egerö, *South African Bantustans. From Dumping Grounds to Battlefronts.* 1991. 46 pp. ISBN 91-7106-315-3

5. Carlos Lopes, *Enough is Enough! For an Alternative Diagnosis of the African Crisis.* 1994. 38 pp. ISBN 91-7106-347-1

6. Annika Dahlberg, *Contesting Views and Changing Paradigms.* 1994. 59 pp. ISBN 91-7106-357-9

7. Bertil Odén, *Southern African Futures. Critical Factors for Regional Development in Southern Africa.* 1996. 35 pp. ISBN 91-7106-392-7

8. Colin Leys and Mahmood Mamdani, *Crisis and Reconstruction – African Perspectives.* 1997. 26 pp. ISBN 91-7106-417-6

9. Gudrun Dahl, *Responsibility and Partnership in Swedish Aid Discourse.* 2001. 30 pp. ISBN 91-7106-473-7

10. Henning Melber and Christopher Saunders, *Transition in Southern Africa – Comparative Aspects.* 2001. 28 pp. ISBN 91-7106-480-X

11. *Regionalism and Regional Integration in Africa.* 2001. 74 pp. ISBN 91-7106-484-2

12. Souleymane Bachir Diagne, et al., *Identity and Beyond: Rethinking Africanity.* 2001. 33 pp. ISBN 91-7106-487-7

13. Georges Nzongola-Ntalaja, et al., *Africa in the New Millennium.* Edited by Raymond Suttner. 2001. 53 pp. ISBN 91-7106-488-5

14. *Zimbabwe's Presidential Elections 2002.* Edited by Henning Melber. 2002. 88 pp. ISBN 91-7106-490-7

15. Birgit Brock-Utne, *Language, Education and Democracy in Africa.* 2002. 47 pp. ISBN 91-7106-491-5

16. Henning Melber et al., *The New Partnership for Africa's development (NEPAD).* 2002. 36 pp. ISBN 91-7106-492-3

17. Juma Okuku, *Ethnicity, State Power and the Democratisation Process in Uganda.* 2002. 42 pp. ISBN 91-7106-493-1

18. Yul Derek Davids, et al., *Measuring Democracy and Human Rights in Southern Africa.* Compiled by Henning Melber. 2002. 50 pp. ISBN 91-7106-497-4

19. Michael Neocosmos, Raymond Suttner and Ian Taylor, *Political Cultures in Democratic South Africa.* Compiled by Henning Melber. 2002. 52 pp. ISBN 91-7106-498-2

20. Martin Legassick, *Armed Struggle and Democracy. The Case of South Africa.* 2002. 53 pp. ISBN 91-7106-504-0

21. Reinhart Kössler, Henning Melber and Per Strand, *Development from Below. A Namibian Case Study.* 2003. 32 pp. ISBN 91-7106-507-5

22. Fred Hendricks, *Fault-Lines in South African Democracy. Continuing Crises of Inequality and Injustice.* 2003. 32 pp. ISBN 91-7106-508-3

23. Kenneth Good, *Bushmen and Diamonds. (Un) Civil Society in Botswana.* 2003. 39 pp. ISBN 91-7106-520-2

24. Robert Kappel, Andreas Mehler, Henning Melber and Anders Danielson, *Structural Stability in an African Context.* 2003. 55 pp. ISBN 91-7106-521-0

25. Patrick Bond, *South Africa and Global Apartheid. Continental and International Policies and Politics.* 2004. 45 pp. ISBN 91-7106-523-7

26. Bonnie Campbell (ed.), *Regulating Mining in Africa. For whose benefit?* 2004. 89 pp. ISBN 91-7106-527-X

27. Suzanne Dansereau and Mario Zamponi, *Zimbabwe – The Political Economy of Decline.* Compiled by Henning Melber. 2005. 43 pp. ISBN 91-7106-541-5

28. Lars Buur and Helene Maria Kyed, *State Recogni-tion of Traditional Authority in Mozambique. The nexus of Community Representation and State Assist-ance.*
2005. 30 pp. ISBN 91-7106-547-4

29. Hans Eriksson and Björn Hagströmer, *Chad – Towards Democratisation or Petro-Dictatorship?*
2005. 82 pp.ISBN 91-7106-549-

30. Mai Palmberg and Ranka Primorac (eds), *Skinning the Skunk – Facing Zimbabwean Futures.*
2005. 40 pp. ISBN 91-7106-552-0

31. Michael Brüntrup, Henning Melber and Ian Taylor, *Africa, Regional Cooperation and the World Market – Socio-Economic Strategies in Times of Global Trade Regimes.* Com-piled by Henning Melber.
2006. 70 pp. ISBN 91-7106-559-8

32. Fibian Kavulani Lukalo, *Extended Handshake or Wrestling Match? – Youth and Urban Culture Celebrating Politics in Kenya.*
2006.58 pp. ISBN 91-7106-567-9

33. Tekeste Negash, *Education in Ethiopia: From Crisis to the Brink of Collapse.*
2006. 55 pp. ISBN 91-7106-576-8

34. Fredrik Söderbaum and Ian Taylor (eds) *Micro-Regionalism in West Africa. Evidence from Two Case Studies.*
2006. 32 pp. ISBN 91-7106-584-9

35. Henning Melber (ed.), *On Africa – Scholars and African Studies.*
2006. 68 pp. ISBN 978-91-7106-585-8

36. Amadu Sesay, *Does One Size Fit All? The Sierra Leone Truth and Reconciliation Commission Revisited.*
2007. 56 pp. ISBN 978-91-7106-586-5

37. Karolina Hulterström, Amin Y. Kamete and Henning Melber, *Political Opposition in African Countries – The Case of Kenya, Namibia, Zambia and Zimbabwe.*
2007. 86 pp. ISBN 978-7106-587-2

38. Henning Melber (ed.), *Governance and State Delivery in Southern Africa. Examples from Botswana, Namibia and Zimbabwe.*
2007. 65 pp. ISBN 978-91-7106-587-2

39. Cyril Obi (ed.), *Perspectives on Côte d'Ivoire: Between Political Breakdown and Post-Conflict Peace.*
2007. 66 pp. ISBN 978-91-7106-606-6

40. Anna Chitando, *Imagining a Peaceful Society. A Vision of Children's Literature in a Post-Conflict Zimbabwe.*
2008. 26 pp. ISBN 978-91-7106-623-7

41. Olawale Ismail, *The Dynamics of Post-Conflict Reconstruction and Peace Building in West Africa. Between Change and Stability.*
2009.52 pp. ISBN 978-91-7106-637-4

42. Ron Sandrey and Hannah Edinger, *Examining the South Africa–China Agricultural Relationship.*
2009. 58 pp. ISBN 978-91-7106-643-5

43. Xuan Gao, *The Proliferation of Anti-Dumping and Poor Governance in Emerging Economies.*
2009. 41 pp. ISBN 978-91-7106-644-2

44. Lawal Mohammed Marafa, *Africa's Business and Development Relationship with China. Seeking Moral and Capital Values of the Last Economic Frontier.*
2009. xx pp. ISBN 978-91-7106-645-9

45. Mwangi wa Githinji, *Is That a Dragon or an Elephant on Your Ladder? The Potential Impact of China and India on Export Led Growth in African Countries.*
2009. 40 pp. ISBN 978-91-7106-646-6

46. Jo-Ansie van Wyk, *Cadres, Capitalists, Elites and Coalitions. The ANC, Business and Development in South Africa.*
2009. 61 pp. ISBN 978-91-7106-656-5

47. Elias Courson, *Movement for the Emancipation of the Niger Delta (MEND). Political Marginalization, Repression and Petro-Insurgency in the Niger Delta.*2009. 30 pp. ISBN 978-91-7106-657-2

48. Babatunde Ahonsi, *Gender Violence and HIV/ AIDS in Post-Conflict West Africa. Issues and Responses.* 2010.
38 pp. ISBN 978-91-7106-665-7

49. Usman Tar and Abba Gana Shettima, *Endangered Democracy? The Struggle over Secularism and its Implications for Politics and Democracy in Nigeria.*
2010. 21 pp. ISBN 978-91-7106-666-4

50. Garth Andrew Myers, *Seven Themes in African Urban Dynamics.*2010. 28 pp.
ISBN 978-91-7106-677-0

51. Abdoumaliq Simone, *The Social Infrastructures of City Life in Contemporary Africa.*
2010. 33 pp. ISBN 978-91-7106-678-7

52. Li Anshan, *Chinese Medical Cooperation in Africa. With Special Emphasis on the Medical Teams and Anti-Malaria Campaign.*
2011. 24 pp. ISBN 978-91-7106-683-1

53. Folashade Hunsu, *Zangbeto: Navigating the Spaces Between Oral art, Communal Security And Conflict Mediation in Badagry, Nigeria.*
2011. 27 pp. ISBN 978-91-7106-688-6

54. Jeremiah O. Arowosegbe, *Reflections on the Challenge of Reconstructing Post-Conflict States in West Africa: Insights from Claude Ake's Political Writings.*
2011. 40 pp. ISBN 978-91-7106-689-3

55. Bertil Odén, *The Africa Policies of Nordic Countries and the Erosion of the Nordic Aid Model: A comparative study.*
2011. 66 pp. ISBN 978-91-7106-691-6

56. Angela Meyer, P*eace and Security Cooperation in Central Africa: Developments, Challenges and Prospects.*
2011. 47 pp ISBN 978-91-7106-693-0

57. Godwin R. Murunga, *Spontaneous or Premeditated? Post-Election Violence in Kenya.*
2011. 58 pp. ISBN 978-91-7106-694-7

58. David Sebudubudu & Patrick Molutsi, *The Elite as a Critical Factor in National Development: The Case of Botswana.*
2011. 48 pp. ISBN 978-91-7106-695-4

59. Sabelo J. Ndlovu-Gatsheni, *The Zimbabwean Nation-State Project. A Historical Diagnosis of Identity and Power-Based Conflicts in a Postcolonial State.*
2011. 97 pp. ISBN 978-91-7106-696-1

60. Jide Okeke, *Why Humanitarian Aid in Darfur is not a Practice of the 'Responsibility to Protect'.*
2011. 45 pp. ISBN 978-91-7106-697-8

61. Florence Odora Adong, *Recovery and Development Politics. Options for Sustainable Peacebuilding in Northern Uganda.*
2011, 72 pp. ISBN 978-91-7106-698-5

62. Osita A. Agbu, *Ethnicity and Democratisation in Africa. Challenges for Politics and Development.*
2011, 30 pp. ISBN 978-91-7106-699-2

63. Cheryl Hendricks, *Gender and Security in Africa. An Overview.*
2011, 32 pp. ISBN 978-91-7106-700-5

64. Adebayo O. Olukoshi, *Democratic Governance and Accountability in Africa. In Search of a Workable Framework.*
2011, 25 pp. ISBN 978-91-7106-701-2

65. Christian Lund, *Land Rights and Citizenship in Africa.*
2011, 31 pp. ISBN 978-91-7106-705-0

66. Lars Rudebeck, *Electoral Democratisation in Post-Civil War Guinea-Bissau 1999–2008.*
2011, 31 pp. ISBN 978-91-7106-706-7

67. Kidane Mengisteab, *Critical Factors in the Horn of Africa's Raging Conflicts.*
2011, 39 pp. ISBN 978-91-7106-707-4

68. Solomon T. Ebobrah, *Reconceptualising Democratic Local Governance in the Niger Delta.*
2011, 32 pp. ISBN 978-91-7106-709-8

www.ingramcontent.com/pod-product-compliance
Lightning Source LLC
Chambersburg PA
CBHW080210300326
41934CB00039B/3443